The Invitation: Wilt Thou?

Through the Love of Jesus Christ

Andy Bowden

Aspect Books

Copyright © 2011 Andy Bowden
ISBN-13: 978-1-57258-720-5 (Paperback)
ISBN-13: 978-1-57258-721-2 (E-book)
Library of Congress Control Number: 2011910587

All scripture quotations, are taken from the King James Version Bible.

Published by
Aspect Books

"Those who are of a contrite heart will receive the message of heaven, and will voice the words of the angel. This is the work of all who have heard the divine invitation. Jesus said to the woman of Samaria what He says to us all, 'If thou knewest the gift of God, and who it is that saith to thee, Give me to drink; thou wouldest have asked of him, and he would have given thee living water. . . . But the water that I shall give him shall be in him a well of water springing up into everlasting life' (John 4:10-14)" (Ellen G. White, *That I May Know Him*, p. 337).

There will be an invitation. The question is will you recognize it, and more importantly, will you accept it or let it pass by.

Andy Bowden

Chapter One

It is the ruin of this world that comes from the blindness. So many are numb and blind from accepting the oppression of him, whom they have chosen to follow into self-inflicted pain.

Look into people's eyes. It doesn't matter what is going on. They could be in the middle of a conversation on their cell phones with a smile on their face, but it is their eyes that give them away. Their eyes are empty, numbed by the pain. There is nothing there. The lives of the lost stream through the streets of the cities and towns on a hectic pace, heading to work or maybe to pick up their children from day care or traveling to some other destinations crammed into their days. They walk through the retail stores with a child on their arm and the cell phone attached to their ear. So often their talk is utter nonsense—talk that fills the void in their minds that would occur if they were to stop for a moment. The child on their arm screams for attention, but he receives only harsh words for interfering.

Why do our children turn out like they do? Could it be our fault? Think of the child on the arm of his parent in the above example. There is the conversation on the cell phone in the middle of a retail store, and there is the scream of the child. Which one gets the attention from the parent? Looking to the extreme, when a young child shoots another, he is crying out for attention. Now the young murderer has the attention he has craved all of his life.

Why do our children turn out like they do? Could it be our fault?

Look at their eyes. It is the eyes that give them away. They are empty eyes numbed by the pain. He has a beautiful wife and two sons. He wants to provide for them, but his days have become endless. The promised work schedule became an empty promise with many excuses as to why and rotating weekends have turned into every weekend. By the time he comes home each night, his family is asleep, and in the mornings he is gone before they awake. The job has become his life.

He struggles with the questions that enter his mind and the decisions he must make. Will he ever find peace and rest? Will he ever be able to slow down and breathe? Will he ever be able to be the kind of husband and father he wants to be? The questions plague him, and his tired eyes stare back at him in the mirror, taunting him and reminding him that he isn't where he wants to be. It seems he never sleeps. In an exhausted trance he pulls his van onto the road that leads him into the darkness.

Look at their eyes. It is the eyes that give them away.

They are empty eyes numbed by the pain. The sixty-year-old man is pushing the broom through the store. The wrinkles are deep and the skin droops down from his eyes. His hands shake as they grip the broom. The company he had worked at for forty years released him. Forty weeks of pay for forty years of work. His severance is gone, and there was no retirement. His wife is at home, too sick to work, and they have no money for the doctor.

The short story on the back page of the newspaper reads of a couple, married thirty-eight years, found in their bed holding each other tight, dead for two days. Many will say "How touching," but the truth from the autopsy will never be written or revealed, because the autopsy will never be done, that would uncover their decision that is just wasn't worth it anymore. Their lives were lost the day he was released from the company that he had given his all to for the woman who he loved so much.

Look at their eyes. It is the eyes that give them away. They are empty eyes numbed by the pain. It is the worker

Why does he take money from the register? Could it be our fault?

behind the counter who looks up at you as you approach but doesn't see you, or seems to stare right through you. He's working for minimum wage, three hundred dollars a week, to pay the rent and take care of his nine-month-old baby. The boss wants more, they always do, but he has nothing else to give. This is the reason he stares right through you. He wishes you would go away so he could at least finish this part of the job, because he will never get done if the customers keep coming up to the counter. One more scream from his boss, and he's out the door, jobless with a hungry infant.

Why does he take money from the register? Could it be our fault? Think of the child on the arm of the parent. Maybe if that child had a child then it would be different. He would be able to give his child the attention he wanted. But he escaped too young, and the baby came so soon, and it needs diapers and food. And what if the baby gets sick? He has to work constantly to make ends almost meet, and he suddenly realizes that he is not paying any attention to his baby, because if he's not working, he passes out from exhaustion on the couch. Wouldn't it be so much easier to rob a store, or maybe a bank? Selling drugs would be easy and profitable, and he could spend much more time with his baby. But too often people who go this route get shot in a robbery gone bad or a drug deal that went sour or are arrested. Now their baby has lost a parent.

What is the answer? Is there an answer to this cold dark-ness that has become the world?

Look at their eyes. It is the eyes that give them away. They are empty eyes numbed by the pain. Heartbreak and empty hearts or hearts that never knew there was something to break over convince many that it is hopeless to try. Many stand in the cold darkness of the eyes of empty pain, seeing no way out and no turning back. What is the answer? Is there an answer to this cold darkness that has become the world?

"For this people's heart is waxed gross,
and their ears are dull of hearing,
and their eyes they have closed;
lest at any time they should see with their eyes
and hear with their ears,
and should understand with their heart,
and should be converted, and I should heal them"
Matthew 13:15, KJV.

Chapter Two

He couldn't remember the last full day he had had off. The job description had read, and was emphasized at his hiring, that weekends were off with the exception of a rotating on call weekend. However, it turned out that every weekend he was on call, and the telephone calls always came. The calls that sent him out and away from his family never seemed to stop coming. It was either other employees on vacation, someone quitting, or someone getting fired, but whatever the reason, the rotating weekend had turned into every weekend. Every time the telephone rang, he felt himself tense inside. He didn't want to answer, but the obligation to the job was the obligation to his family that he would always take care of them, so he always answered the call. Refrigeration, cooling, and heating—that was his trade, and the equipment in the stores that his company serviced was always breaking down.

Last night he had gotten home at about 10:30, and now it was 5:00 a.m., and he was already back on the road. He thought of his two boys who he had not seen in two days. He was always up and gone before they awoke in the morning, and they were fast asleep when he came home at night. His wife was usually drifting off to sleep on the couch, trying to wait up for him so they could spend some time together. He remembered her sleeping so peacefully on the couch last night when he had come home. He had kissed her lightly. She had opened her eyes and smiled at him. "Why don't you go to bed," he had whispered to her.

"Are you coming?" she had asked. He had nodded yes.

He had felt so numb—his body had not wanted to move, so he leaned back on the couch and let out the breath he had not realized he was holding in. His eyes wandered around the room. It seemed like the first time he had ever been in the room. His wife had created a comfortable home filled with pictures of the boys and their wedding. He remembered their special day and felt sadness grip his heart, because it felt as if that day was so long ago. He couldn't remember the last time they had spent any time together, and she never complained. She took care of the house and the boys and supported him in all that he did.

The next thing he remembered was his cell phone ringing on his belt. It had jolted him straight up, but it had taken him a few seconds to understand where he was. His surroundings seemed strange, but the pictures looked familiar. Realization that he was in his own living room tore at his heart, because with the telephone ringing that could only mean he would be leaving soon. He took the call, and with a "yeah" and an "okay," he closed it.

He had no time to eat, only time for a shower. He remembered the morning before, looking in the mirror at his own red eyes looking back at him and a two-day beard. Now those same red eyes stared back at him with a three-day beard covering his face, but he had to go. He looked in to the boy's room where they were sleeping soundly. Walking to each of their beds, he had knelt down and kissed each of their cheeks. How badly he had wanted to wake them and spend the rest of the day just playing with them, running through the house and wrestling as boys do. He had felt the vibration of his cell phone on his belt, but he hadn't bothered to answer it. With one last look back at his boys, he had crossed the hall and quietly went into the bedroom where his wife was sleeping and gently kissed her lips and whispered, "I love you." She had responded likewise in a sleepy whisper.

He smiled as his mind paused on the words his wife has whispered to him. He took a sip of coffee while he

He had thought often of quitting, because it just wasn't worth it. But reality always set in—work was not an option; it was a necessity.

filled his van up with gas. They had been married now for ten years, but he seriously could not remember the last two years. They seemed to be a blur in his mind. The thought saddened him. The gas nozzle clicked off when the tank was filled, and his thoughts returned to his job. He had thought often of quitting, because it just wasn't worth it. But reality always set in—work was not an option; it was a necessity.

He took another drink of the coffee and his cell phone rang again. This time he answered. "Yeah, I'm on my way" was all he said before disconnecting. He had no patience for this right now. The two-lane highway stretched out before him into the darkness. The center dividing lines painted on the dark roads approached him quickly, and they flashed by in his peripheral vision. He felt his eyes zoning in on the fast moving line as he took a long drink from his coffee mug. His eyes stared out onto the road quickly turning under the tires of the van. He began to think of his family again. They were the only reason for his smile these days. His heart longed to spend just one day with them, a day with no telephones and no interruptions. The thought brought tears to his eyes, but he shook them away. For some reason, he remembered a very nice couple he had met recently while working at one store. They had been so nice, and they had even invited him to church. He had said something to them about being so busy, and . . . The bright headlights flashed, bringing his mind back to the road and away from his thoughts.

He finished his coffee, turned on the radio, and then sat back for the ride. The flashing white lines grabbed his attention again. They were almost hypnotizing. He closed his eyes, rubbed them, and then focused back onto the road. The center line kept drawing his eyes. He could see his wife—she was pushing their two sons on the swing set that he had built for them in the backyard. The three of them were all alone—she was pushing them, but she was not smiling. He could see his wife's face, and she seemed so sad. Something was behind her that grabbed his attention, a light so bright it blinded him from seeing them, but it was quickly approaching them from behind.

The blare of the horn opened his eyes. His mind tried desperately to gain control of what was going on. His eyes looked for those familiar faces in the picture, but he could see only the white flashing lines on the road. They were on the wrong side, but he could not figure out why. The blinding flashing light directly in front of him answered the question of why the lines were on the wrong side and what the bright light was behind his wife. The bright lights also answered the question of why his wife had been so sad. These thoughts flashed through his mind, and then he felt it.

The impact was deafening, and it pushed him forward and crushed him amidst the metal of the van. He felt the momentum of the van going the opposite way in which he had been driving. Then for a moment, he felt nothing and heard nothing, and suddenly darkness engulfed him.

Chapter Three

He leaned down with the dustpan in his hand to collect the dirt he had swept into a pile from the aisles of the store. He felt the ache in his knees and back, and it took him a moment to stand back up straight and catch his breath. He dumped the contents of the dustpan into the trash can, tapping it on the edge of the trash can to empty the trash clinging to the dustpan. Lost in his thoughts, he continued tapping though nothing more remained in the dustpan.

After forty years of work, his administrators had called him into the office. The three men were behind the desk, one sitting, and the other two standing on either side of the seated man. The whole situation had seemed strange to him. He felt very uncomfortable in their presence, although he had worked with them for many years. Each of the men had an unsettling look upon their face. Then their words came forth.

They were using words like cutbacks and severance, and the whole situation turned surreal. In a matter of moments, the man sitting down behind the desk had handed him an envelope. He had held the envelope in his hands, looking at it as though he had never seen an envelope before.

"It is forty weeks of pay," the man sitting behind the desk had said. "That should give you time to find something else."

The fogginess had faded away, and he had blankly stated, "Forty weeks, for forty years. What about my retirement?" "Unfortunately, that would only be payable to you if you had worked until you were sixty-five. We are sorry," the man had said.

He remembered how he had stood up and yelled at them in response. "But you are not letting me work until I am sixty-five." Unfortunately they had looked back at

"But you are not letting me work until I am sixty-five."

him with those eyes— look at their eyes; it is the eyes that give them away; they are empty eyes numbed by the pain. He had then felt a hand on his shoulder, and he had looked back to see who had put their hands on him. It had been one of the security guards in the building. He had then turned back to the men behind the desk and said, "How can you do this?" but the grip had tightened on his shoulder.

Returning to the present, he looked into the eyes of the manager of the store in which he now swept floors. "Are you okay?" his manager asked.

The older gentleman could only nod his head.

"Then let's get back to work. You have been standing here for a while, and we don't pay you to stand around and do nothing."

The old man nodded again, and the manager started to walk off. "Hey," the manager turned and said, "we need you to go and clean the men's bathroom up front. Somebody made a terrible stinking mess in there, so go take care of that for me."

He looked at the store manager, and he thought to himself. *I put in forty years of work, and now here I stand as the man who sweeps the floors and cleans the toilets*. He felt his hand loosen around the handle of the broom, wanting to let it drop to the floor, freeing him to walk out the front door of the store and never look back. But the face of his wife flashed before his eyes—she depended upon him to take care of her. She had always depended upon him, and he had always loved taking care of her, because he loved her so. His hand gripped the broom tightly again, and he headed toward the cleaning room, retrieved the cleaning cart, and walked to the men's bathroom.

That night he drove his car into his driveway, shut off the engine, and for a moment, just sat in the car. He looked at the house. The light in the living room was on, and he knew his wife was waiting for him behind the front door. Had he let her down because he could no longer give her what she needed? He felt the tears well in his eyes, and he put his head down and cried.

The tapping on the window was light—he knew it was her. She was always so gentle in everything she did. He turned and looked up into her eyes, and the same tears that filled his eyes, now filled hers. He got out of the car and held her close to him, and for a moment they just stood and cried in the driveway.

"Why are you crying," he asked her.

Had he let her down because he could no longer give her what she needed?

She looked up into his eyes, and through her tears she said, "Because I didn't have anything to cook for you, and I have always had something to cook for you." He pulled her close to him, knowing his wallet was empty. He had no more words to make her feel better. He had always been able to make her feel better, make her feel safe—she had never had to worry, until now. He looked down the street of their neighborhood. The lights shone brightly from the houses. His eyes stopped on the house two doors down, and he remembered seeing the two children playing in the front yard. Their laughter had warmed his heart. The children and their parents had knocked on the door one evening, but life had taken too much from him, and he hadn't bothered to answer the door that evening. He didn't really understand why he even thought about that evening. With his arm around his wife, they walked into the house.

Once inside he went into the bathroom, remembering the pills he had gotten a few years back when he had pulled a muscle in his back. He opened the bottle, and there were still pills inside. He looked at his wife, who was looking back at him. Pouring the pills into the palm of his hand, he separated them. He walked with her into the bedroom and left her there, but he soon returned with two glasses of water. They changed into their pajamas, as they always did; then sitting on the edge of the bed, they swallowed the pills one by one. Lying down on the bed, he held his wife close and said, "I always looked forward to the day when I would retire, and we could spend all of our days together. I am so sorry I could never give you those days."

"You have given me the best days of my life, and I have loved you every minute I have known you," she whispered to him through her tears, which ran down her cheeks. "Now let's go to sleep." He closed his eyes, breathing in her fragrance that he knew so well, he wanted to hold it in one last time, never letting her go. And he did.

Chapter Four

The gun felt heavy in his hands as he pointed it at the man behind the counter, but he held it steady, not wanting to show any fear. He heard himself say, "Fill the bag with the money!" At the same time, the sweat poured down his body. It was so hot, why was he doing this? The man just stared at him, so he pushed the gun over the counter directly into the man's face and said, "I said, fill the bag with the money!"

The man responded now, quickly filling the bag. The bag was soon full, and he grabbed it and ran out the door. He ran down the street as fast as he could. He had left his car a block down from the bank in the parking lot of a busy retail store. He ran across the parking lot, found his car, and locked himself inside. He had forgotten to remove the mask from his face, so people were now looking at him.

He started the engine of the car and drove out of the parking lot. He was driving too fast. He realized that he was calling too much attention to himself, so he slowed down and tried to control himself. Pulling into another crowded parking lot, he parked the car, turned it off, and sat still.

He looked down at his watch and discovered that it was almost three in the afternoon. He only had about ten minutes to pick up his baby boy. He hadn't really had any choice but to leave him with the neighbor. She had invited him in, but he had declined. He had wanted to get the job done quickly before he changed his mind. Her smile had made him hesitate. But something about the woman's smile didn't match the picture in

He had to make the best life for his son as he possibly could.

his mind formed by the smoky stench coming from the apartment. He couldn't stand the thought of the smoke touching his baby or him inhaling the poisonous fumes, but he had no choice.

The baby's mother had run away right after he was born. She was terrified, but she was only fifteen. He had no idea where she was, but he had to take care of the baby. Anyway, he was used to it. His own mother had run away and left him when he was a baby. He had to make the best life for his son as he possibly could. He had tried a normal job, but being only seventeen years old, no one wanted to pay him more than minimum wage, and he found out quickly that he could not survive that way.

He had started stealing from his job, but that caught up with him pretty fast, and he was fired. He had no choice but to do what he was doing now. He had to take care of his son. He had no one to turn to.

Although his mother had not been around to raise him, she now lived in town, but she continued to not care whether she was in his life or not. She was not there for him, and she was definitely not there for her grandson. She was too busy with her own life. He had learned early in life that she only came around and needed him to be her son when she was in between boyfriends. He was not going to subject his son to that kind of life. One way or another he was going to take care of his son.

He snapped back to the present. He had to hurry. He knew the neighbor would not wait for him and would leave his son all alone. But it wasn't far; he would make it on time. He turned into the rundown apartment complex. He hated that he had to expose his son to this place, which was full of drugs and prostitutes. He looked over at the bag of money and smiled, knowing he could leave this place tonight if he wanted. Parking the car, he grabbed the bag and ran to the neighbor's house. She answered, meeting him at the door with his baby boy. She stepped back, inviting him in. He reached for his son and stepped back once his son was in his arms. Reaching into his pocket, he pulled out a twenty-dollar bill and handed it to the woman.

"Oh no, honey," she said, waving off the money. "He was an angel while you were gone."

He stood outside the apartment door looking back at her. Why was she being so friendly? No one in these apartments was ever friendly. He pulled his son tight to him, bringing him close and sniffing his little clothes.

She noticed and said, "I am so sorry. It's my son. I just can't get him to stop smoking."

So many times it was like he had no home of his own.

He stepped a little further back. "Thank you" was all he could say as he turned toward his apartment's door.

"Let me know if you need me again," she said as he walked away.

He only looked back with a smile.

Inside the apartment he ran a bath for his son. He wanted so badly to get the stench off of him. He could feel the tears in his own eyes at the thought of subjecting his son to such things. He wouldn't have to do that anymore. He couldn't stand the thought of just leaving his son anywhere.

He remembered how many times as a child he had slept in a different place. So many times it was like he had no home of his own. He was always sleeping on somebody's couch, or their floor, or if he was lucky, a strange bed. And then, she would be gone again, dropping him off at his dad's house when she no longer needed him or when he got in the way of her new boyfriend. He remembered so many times looking back at her through the window of the car, at her eyes—look at their eyes; it is the eyes that give them away; they are empty eyes numbed by the pain.

He put his son down in the warm soapy water and began to wash him. He smiled down at him, and the little baby boy smiled back at him. He wondered if his mom or dad had ever done this for him. He could not remember a time when it seemed like his mom was happy to see him. In fact, he had no happy memories of his childhood. He remembered his dad always laughing and smiling, but that had been the alcohol making him feel good and not his son.

Rinsing off the baby, he wrapped him in a towel and dried him. Before he dressed him, he pulled him close and held him tight—squeezing as tightly as he dared without hurting him. He wondered what it felt like to be hugged like that, but he knew that when his son got a little older he would find out, because his son would hug him back.

Dressed and warm, the little guy was hungry, so he got out a couple of jars of baby food and set him up in his chair and began to feed him. His son really liked peas. As he fed his son, he thought of his next move. They were definitely leaving this apartment and not looking back. He finished feeding him, got him some apple juice, and then spread out a blanket on the floor so his son could play a little while he looked at what he had in the bag. But when he laid him on the floor, he couldn't help but lie down and play with him.

How many times had he looked at his dad, wishing that just one time he would play with him? He couldn't remember that time ever happening, because it never did. He had asked both his parents, but he had always been told "not now, maybe later." Unfortunately, later had never come. His dad had instead sat there with his friends, laughing, cussing, and drinking. He could see his dad looking back at him with those eyes—look at their eyes; it is the eyes that give them away; they are empty eyes full of self-willed, self-inflicted pain.

He would never tell his son "maybe later." He sat down next to his son and watched him play with a toy. He couldn't take his eyes off of him. He wondered how anyone could be so mean to something so beautiful. How could you not want to give every bit of your attention to something so beautiful? He had never felt happier than he felt right now. It was just him and his son, and that was all either of them would ever need.

Lying on the living room floor, he was suddenly sprayed with splinters of wood from the front door that had just been kicked in. In a matter of seconds, three police officers had jerked him to his feet, pulled his arms behind him, and handcuffed him. The sudden noise and violence startled the baby boy, and he screamed. They began to pull him out the door, but he struggled with them saying, "My baby, my son. What about my son?"

He looked back into the eyes of his crying baby boy. His baby boy was looking back at him. The thoughts flashed through his mind that this would be the last time he would ever see his son. Who was going to take care of him? Where would he sleep tonight? Who was going to feed him in the morning?

The word "NO!!!" was screaming inside of his mind. He was doing the same thing that had been done to him. He had tried so hard, but now his son was going to be alone. He screamed, "What is going to happen to my son?"

"Unless you have someone to call, then he is going to be taken to child welfare," one of the officers said.

All he could think to do, all he could think to say was "My mother lives here in town, can you call her? Please."

Chapter Five

There was a man. He had been crippled for thirty-eight years of his life. The cold darkness of the world stood hopeless before him. Some that knew him had moved him close to a pool of water that was said to have healing powers when the water was stirred at a certain time. However, as it was, you had to be the first in the pool to receive this healing, and his crippled body did not allow him to get into the pool before someone else had beat him in.

With no family and no friends to help him, the man was lost, looking for something that just wasn't there. He lay by the edge of the pool, so close to healing, yet he was unable to, and now lacked the will, to push himself into the pool. His eyes stayed fixed upon the pool, and he watched day by day as others made their way into the pool of healing. It seemed that each one who entered the pool and immersed themselves in the water all came up looking at him—look at their eyes; it is the eyes that give them away; they are empty eyes numbed by the pain. They all left healed but never stayed to help the next. It was all so selfish. They were healed, but they took it with them. However, their healing was from the cold darkness that is this world, and this healing carries with it a price that each must pay that are healed in this way.

He had given up, because although he lay on the edge, the pool was still miles away. Hopeless and crippled, he resigned his life to what it was and what it was going to continue to be. He looked at so many that walked so closely by him wondering if they might be the one who would help roll him into the pool, but most did not even look back at him. He looked upon these men as the ones who could save him, but they only brought continuous disappointments. When hope is gone there is nothing left but the bottom, and when at the bottom there is only one place to look, and that is up.

He looked upon these men as the ones who could save him, but they only brought continuous disappointments.

But one day everything changed for the cripple. One day a Man came by the pool—a gentle Man, a humble Man— and He asked him a question: "Wilt thou be made whole?" (John 5:6).

How often does God ask people this same question? Everyone goes through this life looking at something or someone as the answer to the problems of their life. This crippled man was looking at a pool of water as the answer to the crisis in his life. He wasn't the only one. The story tells us that this pool by the sheep market in Jerusalem had five porches, and around these five porches lay a great multitude of sick people, similar to the crippled man in the story. There were lame, paralyzed, and blind people lying around this pool, and their only hope in life centered around being the first one in the pool at the right time when the water was stirred.

When we read stories like this one in the Bible we read it literally, and the great thing about these stories in the Bible is that they are living stories. Many call the Bible the Living Bible, and this is for a reason. We can read this story as it truly happened, or we can read it as the scenario of our lives. In that instance, those people gathered around the pool suffered from many kinds of sickness. However, let's look at it from another viewpoint.

To say someone is crippled is to automatically think that they can't walk, but think of it another way. A child that is abused may grow up to be crippled in his approach to relationships. If the child is physically abused, the possibility of him growing up and having children of his own and abusing them is very likely to happen. In the child's mind he is crippled to the point that he is not whole in the way God intended him to be when he was created. His mind is crippled, because as a child his parents were not good parents, and through their abuse they crippled his mind. The crippling of a child in this way is sometimes more debilitating than a child who is actually physically crippled and can't walk. In most cases it is easier to overcome physical ailments than to overcome emotional ailments.

In addition to cripples, there were individuals among the multitude around the pool who were paralyzed. This is a serious physical condition. Some paralysis happens

So what is the answer? The answer is in a choice we must make.

from the waist down, while others can't move from the neck down. Now think of those individuals you know who are emotionally paralyzed with fear. There are so many phobias that keep people paralyzed in such a state that many never even come out of their houses.

Also, the blind took up residence with the crowd around the pool. We know what blindness is, but many can see physically, but are blind to the truth. Blindness to the truth is at the core of the problem. Being blind to the truth will lead to crippling paralysis, which binds the multitudes of today.

So what is the answer? The answer is in a choice we must make. The man had been crippled for thirty-eight years. For those thirty-eight years he had looked to the world for the answers of how he would be healed. We don't know how long he had been on the porches of the pool called Bethesda, but we do know that he was defeated in his life. His road had dead-ended at the pool, and it is obvious he would die there.

Yet there was something else at work here. A shadow cast over the spot of the man lying by the pool. It was

34

the shadow of a Man who asked the question, "Wilt thou be made whole?" Of the multitude around the pool, how many would have taken the question seriously? The same question can be asked of the multitude around the "pool" today. The same type of people surround the "pool" today—it is just a two thousand year difference—but the same gentle and humble Man is asking the question, and that is where many got caught up and continue to get caught up today.

Two thousand years ago many wanted a conquering King who would destroy what they disliked most about their world. But He came as a humble servant. He is our King, but He is a King who will kneel down and wash our feet after a day of long travel or a hard day at work. He is a King who listens and answers our prayers. It is all based upon a choice. The choice is to believe

It is all based upon a choice. The choice is to believe and follow or not believe and stay crippled by the pool.

and follow or not believe and stay crippled by the pool. Some may want to stay by the pool just for the chance to roll themselves in before the next person gets in. These are the people who choose to put their money in the lottery for a chance at a million dollars instead of putting it in the offering plate. That was truly what was going on around that pool. The multitudes were all playing their dollars for a chance to be a millionaire.

Of course, the gentle and humble Man of the story is Jesus Christ. He walked directly into the multitude of sinners, to the one man in the multitude who may have been crippled but was certainly not blind. Many on the porches of the pool wouldn't have responded to such a question from a stranger. How would you respond to such a question? Remember, every one of us is around that pool, and Jesus is asking each of us the question "Wilt thou be made whole?". Do we have the eyes to see and the ears to hear? Or are we caught up in what's going on at the pool?

For thirty-eight years the man at the pool had lived a life surrounded by the cold darkness of the world, and within a moment of meeting Jesus Christ, he was on his feet. He made a choice. There is no time so long passed

Let's face it, a world without Jesus Christ is a world without choices.

that we can't turn to Jesus. Jesus has two requests, and the word request is used because Jesus will never force anything upon you. First, He wants your love, your true love. Second, after you have invited Him into your life and He has forgiven you, He will speak five words to you: "Go, and sin no more" (John 8:11).After, the accusers of Mary Magdalene had dropped their stones and one by one walked away from the scene, Jesus spoke to her. "When Jesus had lifted up himself, and saw none but the woman, he said unto her, Woman, where are those thine accusers? hath no man condemned thee? She said, No man, Lord. And Jesus said unto her, Neither do I condemn thee: go, and sin no more" (John 8:10, 11).

Let's face it, a world without Jesus Christ is a world without choices. It is a world where all who live walk blindly day by day in the chaos of Satan's kingdom. In each of us Satan has built up walls and circumstances that blind us from the truth. We put our work, our sicknesses, and our mental anguish at the forefront of our lives. The dollar, the doctors, and the psychiatrists become our gods. We look to them for the answers to the questions of why our lives have turned out like they have.

We are made to believe that it is always someone else's fault, never our own. It is okay to blame your parents or the spouse who said he/she loved you. If it is their fault that you are the way you are, then it is okay for you to remain in the condition you are in, because it is their fault and not yours. They are the ones that need help and need to be fixed.

Such lies rule this world. The truth is that we all need to be fixed—the ones who have hurt us and the ones who have been hurt. Because truthfully speaking, those who have been hurt have hurt others themselves. The porches around the world's "healing pool" are filled with the multitudes of the sick. Sin is the sickness, and the answer does not lie in the pool. When we recognize that this kingdom of Satan is a kingdom of pain and void of love, then and only then will our eyes be open, and we will find the hand of Jesus reaching out to us.

We are all given the opportunity. Jesus will always reach out His hand to each of us and say "Wilt thou be made whole?". But it is for us to see and to reach out and take the hand of Jesus.

The crippled man by the pool of Bethesda accepted the invitation of Jesus, and in that instant his life was changed. The Holy Scriptures tell us what happens when people accept Jesus' outstretched hand. Stories can change; lives can be made new. Revisit, now, the characters of the previous three stories. They didn't have hope before, but read about their transformation when they accept hope and truth.

Chapter Six

He couldn't remember the last full day he had had off. The job description had read, and was emphasized at his hiring, that weekends were off with the exception of a rotating on call weekend. However, it turned out that every weekend he was on call, and the telephone calls always came. The calls that sent him out and away from his family never seemed to stop coming. It was either other employees on vacation, someone quitting, or someone getting fired, but whatever the reason, the rotating weekend had turned into every weekend. Every time the telephone rang, he felt himself tense inside. He didn't want to answer, but the obligation to the job was the obligation to his family that he would always take care of them, so he always answered the call. Refrigeration, cooling, and heating—that was his trade, and the equipment in the stores that his company serviced was always breaking down.

Last night he had gotten home at about 10:30, and now it was 5:00 a.m., and he was already back on the road. He thought of his two boys who he had not seen in two days. He was always up and gone before they awoke in the morning, and they were fast asleep when he came home at night. His wife was usually drifting off to sleep on the couch, trying to wait up for him so they could spend some time together. He remembered her sleeping so peacefully on the couch last night when he had come home. He had kissed her lightly. She had opened her eyes and smiled at him. "Why don't you go to bed," he had whispered to her.

"Are you coming?" she had asked. He had nodded yes.

He had felt so numb—his body had not wanted to move, so leaned back on the couch and let out the breath he had not realized he was holding in. His eyes wandered around the room. It seemed like the first time he had ever been in the room. His wife had created a comfortable home filled with pictures of the boys and their wedding. He remembered their special day and felt sadness grip his heart, because it felt like that day was so long ago. He couldn't remember the last time they had spent any time together, and she never complained. She took care of the house and the boys and supported him in all that he did.

The next thing he remembered was his cell phone ringing on his belt. It had jolted him straight up, but it had taken him a few seconds to understand where he was. His surroundings seemed strange, but the pictures looked familiar. Realization that he was in his own living room tore at his heart, because with the telephone ringing that could only mean he would be leaving soon. He took the call, and with a "yeah" and an "okay" he closed it.

He had no time to eat, only time for a shower. He remembered the morning before looking in the mirror at his own red eyes looking back at him and a two-day beard. Now those same red eyes stared back at him with a three-day beard covering his face, but he had to go. He looked in to the boy's room where they were sleeping soundly. Walking to each of their beds, he had knelt down and kissed each of their cheeks. How badly he had wanted to wake them and spend the rest of the

They had been married now for ten years, but he could not remember the last two years.

day just playing with them, running through the house and wrestling as boys do. He had felt the vibration of his cell phone on his belt, but he hadn't bothered to answer it. With one last look back at his boys, he had crossed the hall and quietly went into the bedroom where his wife was sleeping and gently kissed her lips and whispered, "I love you." She had responded likewise in a sleepy whisper.

He smiled as his mind paused on the words his wife had whispered to him. He took a sip of the coffee while he filled his van up with gas. They had been married now for ten years, but he seriously could not remember the last two years. They seemed to be a blur in his mind. The thought saddened him.

As he finished pumping his gas, he looked up into

the star-filled sky, and he wondered if the man who had spoke this past Saturday was right in what he was saying about those stars. If so, then the One who had put the stars in place, well surely He could... He shook his head.

No, what interest would He have in me? he thought. The gas nozzle clicked off when the tank was filled, and his thoughts returned to his job. He had thought often of just quitting, because it just wasn't worth it. But reality always set in—work was not an option; it was a necessity.

He took another drink of the coffee and his cell phone rang again. This time he answered. "Yeah, I'm on my way" was all he said before disconnecting. He had no patience for this right now. The two-lane highway stretched out before him into the darkness. The center dividing lines painted on the dark roads approached him quickly, and they flashed by in his peripheral vision. He felt his eyes zoning in on the fast moving line and he took a long drink from his coffee mug. His eyes stared out onto the road quickly turning under the tires of the van. He began to think of his family again. They were the only reason for his smile these days. His heart longed to spend just one day with them, a day with no telephones and no interruptions. The thought brought tears to his eyes, but he shook them away. His mind once again unexpectedly returned to the previous Saturday. The man preaching had read something about another man: "He will wipe away all tears." But who was this Man?

They were the nicest couple he had ever met, and he wasn't just saying that when he told his wife about them. He had been down on his hands and knees working on a compressor when they had started talking to him. The couple had invited him and his family to

"He will wipe away all tears." But who was this Man?

come to church on Saturday. He had surprised himself by saying yes, and upon a call to his wife, she had quickly agreed. The thoughts of actual family time had spurred on her decision. It had been so long since they had done anything that if he had said they were going to spend the day digging ditches in the backyard all day, she probably would have agreed.

He finished his coffee, turned on the radio, and then sat back for the ride. The flashing white lines grabbed his attention again. They were almost hypnotizing. He closed his eyes, rubbed them, and then focused back onto the road. The center line kept drawing his eyes. He could see his wife—she was pushing their two sons on the swing set that he had built for them in the backyard. The three of them were all alone—she was pushing them, but she was not smiling. He could see his wife's face, and she seemed so sad. Something was behind her that grabbed his attention, a light so bright it blinded him from seeing them, but it was quickly approaching them from behind.

The blare of the horn opened his eyes. His mind tried

desperately to gain control of what was going on. His eyes looked for those familiar faces in the pictures, but he could see only the white flashing lines on the road. They were on the wrong side, but he could not figure out why. The blinding flashing light directly in front of him answered the question of why the lines were on the wrong side and what the bright light was behind

His mind tried desperately to gain control of what was going on.

his wife. The bright lights also answered the question of why his wife had been so sad. In the waning seconds before impact with the large transport truck, he felt hands upon his own hands, and with a slight turn of the steering wheel, his van moved back to the right side of the road, and the blaring horn of the large truck went speeding by.

He slowed the van and pulled over to the shoulder of the highway. He was breathing hard and was now wide awake. He opened the door and stepped from the van. The truck had disappeared from sight, and no other vehicle was in sight. He looked up at the night sky. The stars filled his eyes, then they began to blur as tears filled his eyes. He dropped to his knees beside the van on the dark highway, remembering the hands that he had felt upon his own inside the van. Looking up he said, "I don't know You, but You just saved me, and I don't know why." He felt something in his heart, and then the vibration on his belt.

"Hello," he said into the telephone. He was still on his knees along the dark highway. "No, I'm not going to be able to make it right now. Yes, that is what I just said. I have been going for weeks, and my family needs me. I am going home," he said just before turning off his telephone.

Two days later he walked out of the office of his immediate supervisor. He smiled as he ran his fingers across his smoothly shaven face. He had just spent two wonderful days with his family. For the last hour, he had talked with his boss. He had sat in the office staring into those eyes looking back at him from across the desk— look at their eyes; it is the eyes that give them away; they are empty eyes full of self-willed, self-inflicted

"I don't know You, but You just saved me, and I don't know why."

pain. But as he had looked into the eyes of his boss who was reprimanding him for not coming to work, he had thought of his wife and his visit with the friendly couple from church. They had told him there was only one explanation for his experience and His name was Jesus. He had recalled that it was Jesus of whom the man had talked about the previous Saturday, saying that "He will wipe away all tears."

The reprimand had stopped in mid-sentence as his

boss had realized that his employee, the one he was disciplining, was smiling at him. Now that his boss had stopped speaking, he had looked directly into his empty eyes and said, "I met Jesus." And through the depths of darkness, a light had sparkled in his boss's eyes.

Chapter Seven

He leaned down with the dustpan in his hand to collect the dirt he had swept into a pile from the aisles of the store. He felt the ache in his knees and back, and it took him a moment to stand back up straight and catch his breath. He dumped the contents of the dustpan into the trash can, tapping it on the edge of the trash can to empty the trash clinging to the dustpan. Lost in his thoughts, he continued tapping though nothing more remained in the dustpan.

After forty years of work, his administrators had called him into the office. The three men were behind the desk, one sitting, and the other two standing on either side of the seated man. The whole situation had seemed strange to him. He felt very uncomfortable in their presence, although he had worked with them for many years. Each of the men had an unsettling look upon their face. Then their words came forth.

They were using words like cutbacks and severance, and the whole situation turned surreal. In a matter of moments, the man sitting down behind the desk had handed him an envelope. He had held the envelope in his hands, looking at it as though he had never seen an envelope before.

"It is forty weeks of pay," the man had said. "That should give you time to find something else."

The fogginess had faded away, and he had blankly stated. "Forty weeks, for forty years. What about my retirement?" "Unfortunately, that would only be payable to you if you had worked until you were sixty-five. We are sorry," the man had said.

He remembered how he had stood up and yelled at them in response. "But you are not letting me work until I am sixty-five." Unfortunately they had looked back at him with those eyes—look at their eyes; it is the eyes that give them away; they are empty eyes numbed by the pain. He had then felt a hand on his shoulder, and he had looked back to see who had put their hands on him. It had been one of the security guards in the building. He had then turned back to the men behind the desk and said, "How can you do this?" but the grip had tightened on his shoulder.

Returning to the present, he looked into the eyes of the manager of the store of which he now swept floors. "Are you okay?" his manager asked.

The older gentleman could only nod his head.

"Then let's get back to work. You have been standing here for a while, and we don't pay you to stand around and do nothing."

The old man nodded again, and the manager started

to walk off. "Hey," the manager turned and said, "we need you to go up and clean the men's bathroom up front. Somebody made a terrible stinking mess in there, so go take care of that for me."

He looked at the store manager, and he thought to himself. *I put in forty years of work and now here I stand as the man who sweeps the floors and cleans the toilets.* He felt his hand loosen around the handle of the broom, wanting to let it drop to the floor, freeing him to walk out the front door of the store and never look back. But the face of his wife flashed before his eyes—she depended upon him to take care of her. She had always depended upon him, and he had always loved taking care of her, because he loved her so. His hand gripped the broom tightly again, and he headed toward the cleaning room, retrieved the cleaning cart, and walked toward the men's bathroom.

Walking up an aisle toward the front of the store, he heard a voice, which at first he thought was not intended for him, but the voice did sound familiar.

"Hey there," the voice spoke again, and he turned and looked. He recognized the face of the young woman who lived two houses down from him with her husband and two young children.

"Hi," he said smiling. Then he turned and continued making his way to the bathroom. About the time he reached the front of the aisle, there was a tap on his shoulder. He turned around.

"How is your sweet wife doing?" It was his neighbor

again. Her smile was so sincere that although he felt at his lowest, he could not help but smile back.

"She is doing fine. Thank you for asking."

"I am so glad that I ran into you today. My husband and I were just talking about how much we enjoyed visiting with you the other day when we stopped by your house. And our kids just love you and your wife. Both my husband's parents and my parents have recently passed away, and our children have really felt that loss. Their relationship was so special. Honestly, our children have never taken to anyone the way they took to you and your wife the other day. Anyway, I am so sorry for

Please Jesus, I pray that my mom and dad will invite our neighbors to church.

rambling on, and I know you have to get back to work, but let me tell you one more thing. We were getting ready to pray the other night and our daughter wanted us to pray for you and your wife because she said you were both so sweet but seemed so sad."

He felt the tears in his eyes as he thought of how honest young children are with their perceptions, and most did little to hide them. He smiled at the young woman but spoke not a word.

"Anyway, right at the end of our prayer, right before we said amen, our little girl said, 'Please Jesus, I pray that my mom and dad will invite our neighbors to church.' So, now Jesus has put you right in front of me, and I am extending an invitation for you and your wife to come visit our church."

The sparkle in the young woman's eyes made him want to say yes, especially as he thought of her dear little daughter. He stood for a moment not knowing

They seemed so happy, and to someone who was so miserable, happy was very hard to tolerate...

exactly what to say. Walking up the aisle five minutes ago he had been lost in the misery of his life. Now a light was shining before him.

"I will talk to my wife about it. Thank you very much. Bye now." He turned and pushed his cleaning cart to the men's bathroom. He stood inside the bathroom waiting for the last person to leave so he could close the bathroom while he cleaned it. As he waited he thought of his neighbors. They had stopped by a couple of days prior to introduce themselves. They seemed so happy, and to someone who was so miserable, happy was very hard to tolerate, but their children had been hard to resist. They were so full of life, not hyper like so many, but just full of life.

The last man left the bathroom, and he blocked off the entrance and got to work. The job was disgusting. He sprayed and cleaned the toilet and the floor around it. His nice encounter with his neighbor was quickly replaced with thoughts of the person who could have left such filth behind without a word of apology. It was obvious the disgusting mess was not an accident, and his thoughts of people in general just got lower. Finally he got up off his knees after scrubbing behind the toilet where the mop could not clean and put everything back in the cleaning cart. He felt so dirty, but what could he do?

That night he drove his car into his driveway, shut off the engine, and for a moment, just sat in the car. He looked at the house. The light in the living room was on, and he knew his wife was waiting for him behind the front door. Had he let her down because he could no longer give her what she needed? He felt the tears well in his eyes, and he put his head down and cried.

The tapping on the window was light—he knew it was her. She was always so gentle in everything she did. He turned and looked up into her eyes, and the same tears that filled his eyes, now filled hers. He got out of the car and held her close to him, and for a moment they just stood and cried in the driveway.

"Why are you crying," he asked her.

She looked up into his eyes, and through her tears she said, "Because I didn't have anything to cook for you, and I have always had something to cook for you." He pulled her close to him, knowing his wallet was empty. He had no more words to make her feel better. He had always been able to make her feel better, make her feel safe—she had never had to worry, until now.

"I'm so sorry," he said.

"You didn't let me finish." His wife stepped back from him and took each of his hands in hers.

At that point I was more lost than I have ever been in my life.

"Three hours ago I was standing in our kitchen with our refrigerator open, staring at the empty shelves and crying because I had just closed the doors on the empty pantry. I was crying, and for a moment I was so lost. At that point I was more lost than I have ever been in my life. For the first time, there was nothing I could do for you. I knew you were coming home to no dinner, and worse than that I knew we had reached the bottom. I stood crying, and I don't know if I said it to myself or out loud, but I said why did it have to end this way? What did we do so bad in our lives? We were always good to everyone. Isn't there someone that can help?"

His wife stopped for a moment and looked into his eyes. The tears were rolling down his face. She reached up and wiped them away.

"And then there was a knock on the front door. I tried to wipe away my tears, and I thought very seriously about not answering the door. But I couldn't help myself. I opened the front door, and there stood our neighbor. She saw the tears in my eyes, and I only saw love in hers. I stepped back from the door, and she walked in, sat down her bags and embraced me with her kindness. She kissed me on the cheek and looked into my eyes. She then told me about Jesus and shared with me a Bible text. In Matthew 11:28-30, Jesus said, 'Come unto me, all ye that labour and are heavy laden,

This gift is not from us but from our Father who loves each one of us.

and I will give you rest. Take my yoke upon you, and learn of me; for I am meek and lowly in heart: and ye shall find rest unto your souls. For my yoke is easy, and my burden is light.' "She stepped back and held my hands like I am holding yours now, and she asked if there was anything she could do. I told her no. I told her that I would be okay and you would be home soon. She squeezed my hands and told me she would see me again soon. She then said goodbye and left. I looked at the two bags she had left behind, and I walked over to them to pick them up and get them to her before she had gotten too far away, but there was a note lying on top of one of the bags."

She pulled a piece of paper from her pocket and read it to her husband. "I didn't expect you to answer the door, or if you did I thought that you might not accept this gift, but I wanted very much to give you this food from the love of Jesus. Times are so hard now, and we must love one another and take care of one another. I pray that you will accept this food as our loving gift for you both. This gift is not from us but from our Father who loves each one of us. Thank you for being our neighbor."

He pulled her close to him, and as he hugged her tight, his eyes drifted up into the evening sky, and with his arm around her, they walked into the house. His wife had set a beautiful table with dinner for two from the love of their neighbors.

His wife looked at him and said, "You have given me the best days of my life, and I have loved you every minute I have known you." Tears were running down her cheeks. "Now let's have a nice dinner together and talk about visiting that church our wonderful neighbors attend."He closed his eyes and pulled her as close as he could, breathing in her fragrance that he knew so well, he wanted to hold it in forever, never letting her go. And he did, as he always had.

Chapter Eight

The gun felt very heavy in his hands. He had borrowed it from a friend, saying he needed it for protection. The apartments he lived in with his infant son were filled with drug dealers, prostitutes, and the elderly poor. So, saying it was for protection wasn't really a lie, but it wasn't the reason he needed the gun. He had just lost his job—his minimum wage job—for stealing. In his mind he really had no other choice but to steal to support his baby. What else could he do? He couldn't live on minimum wage. It barely paid for the day care and food. How could he pay the rent if he didn't supplement his pay.

But he had gotten caught, and by luck he wasn't sitting in jail right now with the state coming to take his baby. Now, looking at the gun, he went over his plan. He needed money, and not just a little. He wanted enough to get his son out of these surroundings, which were so dangerous to his young life. He had seen so many times on television bank robberies where the bank robber got away and lived so well. Why couldn't he do the same?

Suddenly he heard crying come from the one bedroom that the apartment contained, and as if the infant would recognize the gun if he saw it, he opened a drawer in the kitchen and hid the gun in it. He went with a smile to pick up his son. The infant boy quieted as his dad picked him up and held him tight. He could feel the easy breath of his son in his ear as he rested his little head upon his shoulder. How many times as a boy had he longed to feel the embrace of at least one of his parents?

He remembered how many times as a child he had slept in a different place. So many times it was as if

He had no happy memories ...

he had no home of his own. He had often slept on somebody's couch or their floor or if he was lucky a strange bed. And then his mother would be gone again, dropping him off at his dad's house when she no longer needed him or when he got in the way of her new boyfriend. He remembered so many times looking back at her through the window of the car, at her eyes—look at their eyes; it is the eyes that give them away; they are empty eyes full of self-willed, self-inflicted pain.

He decided it would be a good time to bathe his son. He ran the bath water and laid the baby down on a towel to remove his clothes and diaper. The baby looked up into his dad's eyes with a contentment that melted his heart. He put his son down in the warm soapy water and began to wash him. He smiled down at him, and the little baby boy smiled back at him. He wondered if his mom or dad had ever done this for him. He could not remember a time when it seemed like his mom was happy to see him. In fact, he had no happy memories of his childhood. He remembered his dad always laughing and smiling, but that had been the alcohol making him feel good and not his son.

Rinsing off the baby, he wrapped him in a towel and dried him. Before he dressed him, he pulled him close and held him tight—squeezing as tightly as he dared without hurting him. He wondered what it felt like to be hugged like that, but he knew that when his son got a little older he would find out, because his son would hug him back. He thought of the love that this little guy's mother was missing, and he thought of his own mother again.

The baby's mother had run away right after he was born. She was terrified, but she was only fifteen. He had no idea where she was, but he had to take care of the baby. Anyway, he was used to it. His own mother had run away and left him when he was a baby. He had to make the best life for his son as he possibly could.

He had tried a normal job, but being only seventeen years old, no one wanted to pay him more than minimum wage. He had no choice but do to do what he was doing now. He had to take care of his son. He had no one to turn to.

Although his mother had not been around to raise him, she now lived in town, but she continued to not care whether she was in his life or not. She was not there for him, and she was definitely not there for her grandson. She was too busy with her own life. He had learned early in life that she only came around and needed him to be her son when she was in between boyfriends. He was not going to subject his son to that kind of life. One way or another he was going to take care of his son.

Dressed and warm, the little guy was hungry, so he got out a couple of jars of baby food and set him up in his chair and began to feed him. His son really liked peas. As he fed his son, he thought of his next move. They were definitely leaving this apartment and not looking back. He finished feeding him, got him some apple juice, and then spread out a blanket on the floor so his son could play a little, giving himself some time to make his plan. But when he laid him on the floor, he couldn't help but lie down and play with him. How many times had he looked at his dad, wishing that just one time he would play with him?

He couldn't remember that time ever happening, because it never did. He had asked both his parents, but he had always been told "not now, maybe later." Unfortunately, later had never come. His dad had instead sat there with his friends, laughing, cussing, and drinking. He could see his dad looking back at him with those eyes—look at their eyes; it is the eyes that give them away; they are empty eyes full of self-willed, self-inflicted pain.

He would never tell his son "maybe later." He sat down next to his son and watched him play with a toy.

He couldn't take his eyes off of him. He wondered how anyone could be so mean to something so beautiful. How could you not want to give every bit of your attention to something so beautiful? He had never felt happier than he felt right now. It was just him and his son, and that was all either of them would ever need.

He did not want to look bad in his son's eyes.

He checked the clock on the wall and knew he had to get going if he was going to do this. He had talked to the neighbor across the hallway about keeping his son for about two hours. He didn't know her that well, but he really had no choice. There had to be money for food tomorrow, and the rent was coming due, and if everything went according to his plans, he would be paying rent in a safer place. He gathered a couple of toys and diapers. Before he picked up his son, he went into the kitchen and removed the gun from its hiding place. He tucked it in his belt at the small of his back, not wanting his son to see it. He did not want to look bad in his son's eyes.

He walked back in to where his son laid on the floor playing, holding one of his toys up in front of his face. He stopped for a minute to watch, but his eyes went to the clock again. He picked up his son, and closing the door behind them, walked across the hall and knocked on the neighbor's door.

The Invitation: Wilt Thou?

The door opened, and the woman smiled at him and his son. "Come in, come in," she said with such a sweet voice and nice smile. She made him smile and relax a little about leaving his son with her.

"Come in and sit down for a few minutes so you can tell me any instructions I need to know while you are gone. Will you be gone long?"

"No, only about two hours," he answered. He told her that he had a fresh diaper and had also just eaten, so he should be good for a couple of hours. "In fact," he said, "he may go back to sleep again."

The stench of smoke was strong inside the apartment. He pulled his son close, sniffing his clothes while his eyes searched the room for the cigarette.

"I'm sorry, honey, that is my son in his room. I just can't seem to get through to him about smoking. I will make sure he stays in his room while your son is here," she said.

"Now what about you?" she asked. "What do you have planned for these couple of hours?"

A silence came over the room. He looked at his son and then down at his feet.

"I know there are no two-hour shifts at work, and it won't be much of a date if you are planning on being back in two hours. I have a mother's instinct. I see the way you take care of your son, how you love him, and I'm guessing that in your heart you are thinking that what you are about to do is the best thing for him. But

I'm telling you right now, you are wrong."

Her words hung in the air, and he lifted his head from staring down at his shoes and looked into her

Something was pulling at his heart, a feeling he had never felt.

eyes. He then looked down at his son who was looking back at him. There was something going on here. Something was pulling at his heart, a feeling he had never felt. As he held out his son to his neighbor, he said, "I will be back. I just have some business I need to take care of."

She took his small son from him, but as he turned to leave, she held his hand, and he felt a small hand wrap around his left index finger. He looked down, and his son was holding his finger and looking into his eyes. A little tear ran down his son's cheek. No sounds of a coming cry, just a tear. He looked at the woman who was looking at his son, and when the tear fell, she turned and looked at him.

"What are you going to do, son?"

The word son squeezed his heart. How long had he waited for someone to call him that. He looked at her.

"I can tell you what you can do. I just cooked some lunch, and I have plenty. Stay here and we can talk about your plans, and if all goes well, maybe you can go with me to church tonight. If you feel like leaving after lunch, then you can go, and I will care for your boy. It is your choice."

He looked at his son in her arms. A smile came over the baby's face—his eyes had never left his dad. He looked at the woman and said, "I'll stay."

Chapter Nine

Life is so precious. It was in the Garden of Eden that God gave us life. He formed us out of the dust and breathed life into us. His intentions for us were eternal, and He gave us paradise on earth. In the perfection of the garden, there was God and God alone. He was the world and all that was in it. But this perfection was ripped at the seam, and Satan, with his fallen heart, sought to be the one in whom Adam and Eve worshipped. Paradise now had a gaping hole and all those fallen from heaven who had followed Satan into sin rushed in. It was no longer a world of God and God alone. Adam and Eve's choice changed things forever.

This is where each of us sit, right in the middle of a choice to be made. We are being called by the love of God, but the noise of Satan surrounds us, confuses us, and leads us into sin. Among the noise and confusion there is a light shining, and we can see it if we will just open our eyes for a moment. The invitation is always there no matter where we are in our lives.

The perfect story began in the Garden of Eden, as each of our lives begins in the arms of our parents, but there are no more perfect stories because we are born into a world of sin. Satan has made sure of this.

The Invitation: Wilt Thou?

Everyone walks through life carrying their own story and making their own eternal choices. The choices everyone makes are based off of their life story and the foundation their life is built upon.

We were all children at one time. This is where it started for each of us. We all had parents who were our examples. What have we experienced in our

Everyone walks through life carrying their own story and making their own eternal choices.

lives? What has brought us to this point in our lives? What has shaped us? What is it that has made us the teenager we are, the young adult we are, the middle-aged parent we are, or the retired grandparent? What are we doing in our lives? How we are affecting our children?

There is a boy who will learn about women from the pages of an adult magazine, about alcohol every time he opens a beer for his dad, and cigarettes every time he lights one for his father.

There is a girl who will learn about marriage from her mother with a black eye, a mother who piles on the make-up to attract the man at the bar who will blacken her eye, the same man who will touch the little girl not like a dad should.

The effect of parents on their children, both good

and bad, is something children have to deal with for the rest of their lives.

For example, he was six years old. His parents had made some bad decisions that had affected their relationship. These bad decisions had led to a final decision to break up. Actually, it was the father of the boy who had decided to break up the family. The two had never married, but they had brought a baby into the world, and there was no doubting their love for the boy. However, alcohol, drugs, and adultery all played a part in this terrible breakup. Sadly, the young boy had seen it all.

This story is an obvious picture of going against the will of God. However, can the parents be blamed, because they did not know God? In this story, though the sin is so evident, God's love is also very evident. Where there is sin, there will also be the shining light of God. The parents of the young boy had begun their relationship in sin, and she became pregnant. While wrong, this became a beautiful opportunity for God's light to shine in their lives through the birth of their baby boy. The parents' love was never lacking, but God's love in the relationship was, and the relationship ended.

Out of the break up God's light finally shone upon the mother, and she met Jesus for the first time. Unfortunately, when she tried to share the good news with the father of her young son, he was not ready. The father continued on his path of wrong decisions, and his selfishness blinded him to the fact that he was hurting his little boy.

God strengthened the mother, and though they struggled, God saw them through. The mother and

His life was nothing but sin, but the light of God was beginning to split the darkness.

son prayed together because they had finally seen the will of God in their lives. They prayed, and the mother saw the father of her child as her husband, and the boy prayed for his parents to be together again. She became a wonderful mother, as seen by the actions of the boy. At times she felt helpless, but at those times she threw herself upon the mercy of Jesus and let Him work. Through the prayers of the mother and son, the Holy Spirit touched the father's heart, and he made contact with the mother. As they talked, she asked him if he would like to see their son. She told him how much their son missed him. The father agreed. Although he had distanced himself from them and was wallowing in his selfish sin, there was something going on, a light shining somewhere inside of him. His life was nothing but sin, but the light of God was beginning to split the darkness. They agreed on a place to meet.

As the father sat waiting for them to arrive, he felt an excitement building, but also a fear. He knew he had hurt his son by leaving them the way he had. He thought of all the bad decisions he had made, and the sin. His fear was that his son would not want anything to do with him, and who would blame him. He saw them enter, and for the first time in quite a while, he saw his son. He had grown. His son saw him, and the father's heart leaped when he saw the excitement in his sons face. The father could see the little boy's first reaction was to break away and run to him, but something stopped him. His little eyes looked up at his mother, and he stayed close to her. It was at that point that the dad saw the mother she had become. As they came up to the father, the little boy held himself back. When they

How many tears had the boy cried, and how many prayers had he sent up to God?

got close enough, the dad heard the mother say, "Go ahead," and the boy ran into the arms of his father.

The boy had seen all the sin. He had experienced all the pain of the sin, but he himself had never been guilty of the sin. All the sin of the relationship, the bad decisions and the selfishness, was upon the shoulders of this little boy. Yet, in an instant all of that sin disappeared. The boy had taken it all upon himself, and in a moment, forgiveness came into his heart, and father and son embraced. How many tears had the boy cried, and how many prayers had he sent up to God? As the father held his son in his arms, the Holy Spirit convicted his heart, and he knew that he was experiencing the love of God.

The Invitation: Wilt Thou?

There are so many ways we as parents can determine and influence the lives of our children. What a tremendous, yet beautiful responsibility God has given us.

There was a little girl just five years old. She was the daughter of happily married parents. She has grown up knowing Jesus, because her parents had taught her all about Him. Her father works a lot, and his daughter misses him so much that when he comes home she runs and clings to him, wanting every possible minute she can have with him.

However, he is tired. The week has been long, and though he wants to spend time with his little girl, selfishness takes over, and as her questions come and stories of her day spill out of her mouth, his impatience rises up. If he could only have a few minutes of silence, then everything would be all right. The little girl makes the mistake of asking the same question twice, and her father's patience can hold back no longer. He doesn't accept this at work, and he will not accept this at home. His voice rises. She is not used to this, and his loud voice breaks her heart. She begins to cry because her heart is breaking, and her father grows even more impatient. His words are harsh. She runs off crying.

She had waited for him all day, longing to tell him everything about her day. But he pushed her away. Everything that the father had been carrying that day he placed upon the shoulders of his little girl. His anger, tiredness, and impatience from the long hours of work came down upon her like the sin of this world upon Jesus. And it is because of Jesus that the father knew what he had just done. The world had come in the door of his house, and the world did not belong in his house—the house that Jesus had blessed them with—and he had

Jesus never looks upon us with contempt, only love.

just lashed out at those whom he loves so much. He called his little girl to him. She came back into the room, and when her father held out his arms to her, there was no hesitation on her part. She went directly into her father's arms. Everything was forgotten. Everything she had just endured for her father was forgiven in a moment's time.

The father whispered the words "I am so sorry. Do you forgive me?" He could feel the nod of her head as he held her tight against him.

If you look into the stories of these two young children, you will see the forgiveness of Jesus Christ. Jesus went to the cross with every one of our sins upon Him, and as He hung upon that cross, He looked down at those who had beat Him. And although they continued to yell at Him and curse Him and accuse Him, He looked upon them with such love, and He spoke these words: "Father, forgive them; for they know not what they do" (Luke 23:34).

Jesus never looks upon us with contempt, only love.

The Invitation: Wilt Thou?

It is very hard to understand or even accept that anyone could have only love in their heart, but Jesus does. It is His love that forgives and forgets our sins. His arms are always open to receive us. Just like the love of our children.

Think about the following passage that is taken from *Patriarchs and Prophets*. Ellen White writes: "Of Enoch it is written that he lived sixty-five years, and begat a son. After that he walked with God three hundred years. During these earlier years Enoch had loved and feared God and had kept His commandments. He was one of the holy line, the preservers of the true faith, the progenitors of the promised seed. From the lips of Adam he had learned the dark story of the Fall, and the cheering one of God's grace as seen in the promise; and he relied upon the Redeemer to come. But after the birth of his first son, Enoch reached a higher experience; he was drawn into a closer relationship with God. He realized more fully his own obligations and responsibility as a son of God. And as he saw the child's love for its father, its simple trust in his protection; as he felt the deep, yearning tenderness of his own heart for that first-born son, he learned a precious lesson of the wonderful love of God to men in the gift of His Son, and the confidence which the children of God may repose in their heavenly Father. The infinite, unfathomable love of God through Christ became the subject of his meditations day and night; and with all the fervor of his soul he sought to reveal that love to the people among whom he dwelt" (p. 84).

If we follow the example of Enoch and meditate upon the love of Jesus, our love for our children, as well as humanity, will change the lives of so many.

Chapter Ten

"For God so loved the world, that he gave his only begotten Son, that whosoever believeth in Him should not perish, but have everlasting life" (John 3:16).

"For I came down from heaven, not to do mine own will, but the will of him that sent me" (John 6:38).

God's Holy Word is a love story. It is a story of unconditional, unwavering, and even relentless love. It is a love that knows no boundaries, yet it is a love that can only be expressed in one way. It is a story written for each of us. Jesus speaks to us saying, "I came down from heaven, that whoever believes will be saved." This is the path of the love of the Holy Bible. It starts with believing.

But why does God love us so much? His beautiful Eden was tainted by the darkness of our sin, and God had to take it away from us and protect it. Then we darkened His entire world with our sin, and He had to cleanse this world with a Flood. Thousands of years later we live in the filth of sin, yet the voice of God can still be heard. God's promise of John 3:16 still stands. He has not and will not change. But the question remains; why does God love us so much? He loves us so much that

He gave the life of His only Son so that we would not have to suffer the death of sin. Though we are the very reason for the trouble we are in, God gave us a way out. Not a free pass, but a gift of love, and He gave it to us in the form of His only Son. We have to let that sink in and then ask the question of ourselves, "Would I give my child's life so that everyone else might live?" Your first response might be "Does it have to be my child?"

God did not respond that way. In fact, He acted before the question was ever asked. What kind of love is this that God so willingly gives to each of us? It seems so deep, a love unfathomable to us. What kind of love

What kind of love is this that God so willingly gives to each of us?

is this that is so forgiving, though we know the pain we must cause this love, yet through the pain it seems to forget what we have just done to cause the pain. How can this be?

"But Jesus said, Suffer little children, and forbid them not, to come unto me: for of such is the kingdom of heaven" (Matt. 19:14).

Can the answer to our question be in this verse from Matthew? Jesus uses the words "little children" and "such is the kingdom of heaven." Is the kingdom of God in our little children?

Jesus said, "Little children . . . such is the kingdom

of heaven." How beautiful to think of the infinite God and His love for us. We think of a love that we can't reach, that we can't possibly give. Surely the love of God, the One who created this universe, is out of our reach. He can love us that way, but we couldn't possibly love like He does. And then the words of Jesus speak

It is our love that He wants.

to us, and we see our little child before us loving us unconditionally, putting away all faults that we might have.

There are days when we are so tired and so impatient, days when all we want to do is come home and sit down and rest. Those selfish feelings try so hard to control our lives and push our little children away, and then we look down at their little faces and the love of God is looking right back at us. This is how God looks at each of us as we stumble through our lives. When we fall before Him in sin, God looks to His only Son, and it is the hand of Jesus that reaches out and brings us back to our feet. And if we look at Him with our shame, He embraces us, already forgiving and forgetting what we have done. It is our love that He wants. It is the same love our children want and are giving us.

"Suffer the little children" are the words spoken by our Lord Jesus. Though the Holy Scripture tells us we are born into sin, our children are born with an innocence about them in which they are blameless and spotless. It is the influence of their parents and this world that pollutes their lives with sin. Though the child has not sinned, they will bear the weight of their parents' sin upon them. They see every abuse or addiction, hear every harsh word, see every wrong action, and feel every emotion their parents feel in one way or another. A parent may never realize the effect of their sin upon their children, but do the parents realize the effect of their sin upon Jesus?

"At the same time came the disciples unto Jesus, saying, Who is the greatest in the kingdom of heaven?

Jesus leaves no doubt that children are of the kingdom of God, and to harm one is to bring judgment.

And Jesus called a little child unto him, and set him in the midst of them, And said, Verily I say unto you, Except ye be converted, and become as little children, ye shall not enter into the kingdom of heaven. Whosoever therefore shall humble himself as this little child, the same is greatest in the kingdom of heaven. And whoso shall receive one such little child in my name receiveth me. But whoso shall offend one of these little ones which believe in me, it were better for him that a millstone were hanged about his neck, and that he were drowned in the depth of the sea. . . . Take heed that ye despise not one of these little ones; for I say unto you, That in heaven their angels do always behold the face of my

Father which is in heaven" (Matt. 18:1-10).

We must see the examples and the warnings that God shows us in His Holy Word. By reading the words of Jesus in the Gospel of Matthew, we must study how Jesus looks at children. Jesus leaves no doubt that

Jesus came to show us what a sinless life is...

children are of the kingdom of God, and to harm one is to bring judgment. Jesus was speaking to Nicodemus when He said,

"Verily, verily, I say unto thee, Except a man be born again, he cannot see the kingdom of God" (John 3:3).

When we are born, we are a child. So, to be born again means to become like a child again. Take John 3:3, which tells us we can't see the kingdom of God unless we are born again, and compare it to Matthew 19:14, which tells us that children are the kingdom of God. What do we discover? The kingdom of God is in the lives of our children, and to enter into the kingdom we must accept Jesus' invitation and become His child.

Not only has God given us His Holy Word to study and follow, but He has also given us a perfect example of Himself in our children. When God puts a little child into our arms, which can only happen through His grace and mercy in our lives, a picture of His perfect love and forgiveness is presented to us. It is our example that darkens their young lives and shows them exactly what sin is. Jesus came to show us what a sinless life is, and He gave us our children, not only as a blessing, but to give us a true picture of His love and forgiveness.

Refer back to the children spoken of in Chapter Nine, and look at how our children love us as parents. Think of the little boy and how he ran into the arms of his father. The boy dumped the sin that had been the reason, the wall between them, and it was the grace and mercy inside that little boy that made the sin disappear. Think of the little girl who only wanted some precious time with her father but was met full force with the sin that lay upon the shoulders of her father. She took the full frontal assault of her father's day in the world of sin. But at the sound of her father's gentle voice, the one she knew so well, every harsh word and action, and every memory of her father's raised voice, is left behind as she jumps into her father's arms.

Isaiah wrote about Jesus' character and His love and sacrifice for us: "For he shall grow up before him as a tender plant, and as a root out of a dry ground: he hath no form nor comeliness; and when we shall see him, there is no beauty that we should desire him. He is despised and rejected of men; a man of sorrows, and acquainted with grief: and we hid as it were our faces from him; he was despised, and we esteemed him not.

"Surely he hath borne our griefs, and carried our sorrows: yet we did esteem him stricken, smitten of God, and afflicted. But he was wounded for our transgressions, he was bruised for our iniquities: the chastisement of our peace was upon him; and with his stripes we are healed. All we like sheep have gone astray; we have turned every one to his own way; and the LORD hath laid on him the iniquity of us all.

"He was oppressed, and he was afflicted, yet he opened not his mouth: he is brought as a lamb to the slaughter, and as a sheep before her shearers is dumb, so he openeth not his mouth. He was taken from prison and from judgment: and who shall declare his generation? for he was cut off out of the land of the living: for the transgression of my people was he

How many times have you allowed the sin of this world to take over your life, even for a day?

stricken. And he made his grave with the wicked, and with the rich in his death; because he had done no violence, neither was any deceit in his mouth.

"Yet it pleased the LORD to bruise him; he hath put him to grief: when thou shalt make his soul an offering for sin, he shall see his seed, he shall prolong his days, and the pleasure of the LORD shall prosper in his hand. He shall see of the travail of his soul, and shall be satisfied: by his knowledge shall my righteous servant justify many; for he shall bear their iniquities. Therefore will I divide him a portion with the great, and he shall divide the spoil with the strong; because he hath poured out his soul unto death: and he was numbered with the transgressors; and he bare the sin of many, and made intercession for the transgressors" (Isaiah 53:2-12).

How many times have you allowed the sin of this world to take over your life, even for a day? When we succumb to this temptation, the results are shameful and we pull away from turning and facing Him. Fortunately, His love is strong and because He is calling you, you turn around, and there He stands, our Lord Jesus Christ. He knows when we sin, because He feels every sin of this world. The pain of every sin of the world is upon Him, and because of this we can see the depths of His love for us. Jesus feels each sin, but if with a sincere heart we cry out to Him, He pulls us into His loving embrace as we speak the words "Forgive me, Father," and He bears the weight of what we have done. It is then that we look up into His eyes, and there is no trace of what we have done looking back us. Only love. The pure love of your child looking to you is the pure love of Jesus looking at us.

Chapter Eleven

The "tender plant" that the Prophet Isaiah prophecies of in Isaiah 53 is the Man whose shadow cast across the man at the pool of Bethesda. It is the same shadow that casts across your life.

Thinking back to the illustrations of the father who held his son in his arms after so many bad decisions in his life and the father who held his little girl in his arms after shifting the weight of the world from his shoulders to hers, ask yourself one question.

What is God showing us in our children?

"For God sent not his Son into the world to condemn the world; but that the world through him might be saved" (John 3:17).

When our children see or experience the sin in our lives, there is no condemnation, only forgiveness waiting for us to ask of them. Our children are longing for our love, and so is Jesus. Do you see the saving grace of Jesus in the eyes of the child you love so very much? Our Lord Jesus is teaching us through the very special gift that He has given us in our children.

Every time we taint our children with sin and they still run into our arms, they are responding to us as

Jesus responded to Mary Magdalene and as He does to each of us who ask:"Neither do I condemn thee: go, and sin no more" (John 8:11).

How are our decisions affecting our children's lives now, and their future lives?

However, there is a point in a child's life when they can take no more of our sin because they begin to experience their own sin from our example as parents. How often does this happen in every household every day?

We must look at the decisions we are making in our lives. How are our decisions affecting our children's lives now, and their future lives? What are we saying in front of our children, and what are our actions that they see?

What we put into their lives now will prepare them for what will confront them in the future. Things in life will not always work out perfectly. There will always be decisions for them to make. It is all in the way that they make their decisions. When confronted with a job that takes them away from their family, physically runs them in the ground, and literally becomes life threatening, what decision do they make? As our children go through life, are they prepared to stand firm when they lose a critical part of their lives, like a job they thought would support them throughout their career? Have they built a foundation upon the Rock that is Jesus Christ? How will they handle the struggles of this world? Will they see it as the end of their life? Are they prepared to turn into young adults who have their attention upon God, school, career, and the future and not where the formula and the next box of diapers are coming from?When the path gets trampled before us and the world comes down upon us, do we know who to turn to? Do our children know?

Consider this: "Train up a child in the way he should go: and when he is old, he will not depart from it" (Prov. 22:6).Now read John 16:25-33: "These things have I spoken unto you in proverbs: but the time cometh, when I shall no more speak unto you in proverbs, but I shall shew you plainly of the Father. At that day ye shall ask in my name: and I say not unto you, that I will pray the Father for you: For the Father himself loveth you, because ye have loved me, and have believed that I came out from God. I came forth from the Father, and am come into the world: again, I leave the world, and go to the Father. His disciples said unto him, Lo, now speakest thou plainly, and speakest no proverb. Now are we sure that thou knowest all things, and needest not that any man should ask thee: by this we believe that thou camest forth from God. Jesus answered them, Do ye now believe? Behold, the hour cometh, yea, is now come, that ye shall be scattered, every man to his own, and shall leave me alone: and yet I am not alone, because the Father is with me. These things I have spoken unto you, that in me ye might have peace. In the world ye shall have tribulation: but be of good cheer; I have overcome the world."When the shadow of Jesus Christ cast itself upon your life, He extended the invitation to you.

Jesus is asking, "Do ye now believe?"

During the time that Jesus spent in this world, He was in constant communion with God. He spent many hours in prayer, wanting only to do the will of the Father. When the time was drawing near and Jesus knew His death was fast approaching, He took the time to send up the most beautiful prayer.

Jesus is asking, "Do ye now believe?"

"These words spake Jesus, and lifted up his eyes to heaven, and said, Father, the hour is come; glorify thy Son, that thy Son also may glorify thee: As thou hast given him power over all flesh, that he should give eternal life to as many as thou hast given him. And this is life eternal, that they might know thee the only true God, and Jesus Christ, whom thou hast sent. I have glorified thee on the earth: I have finished the work which thou gavest me to do. And now, O Father, glorify thou me with thine own self with the glory which I had with thee before the world was.

"I have manifested thy name unto the men which thou gavest me out of the world: thine they were, and thou gavest them me; and they have kept thy word. Now they have known that all things whatsoever thou hast given me are of thee. For I have given unto them the words which thou gavest me; and they have received them, and have known surely that I came out from thee, and they have believed that thou didst send me. I pray for them: I pray not for the world, but for them which thou hast given me; for they are thine. And all mine are thine, and thine are mine; and I am glorified in them.

"And now I am no more in the world, but these are in the world, and I come to thee. Holy Father, keep through thine own name those whom thou hast given me, that they may be one, as we are. While I was with them in the world, I kept them in thy name: those that thou gavest me I have kept, and none of them is lost, but the son of perdition; that the scripture might be fulfilled. And now come I to thee; and these things I speak in the world, that they might have my joy fulfilled in themselves. I have given them thy word; and the world hath hated them, because they are not of the world, even as I am not of the world. I pray not that thou shouldest take them out of the world, but that thou shouldest keep them from the evil. They are not of the world, even as I am not of the world. Sanctify them through thy truth: thy word is truth. As thou hast sent me into the world, even so have I also sent them into the world. And for their sakes I sanctify myself, that they also might be sanctified through the truth.

"Neither pray I for these alone, but for them also which shall believe on me through their word; That they all may be one; as thou, Father, art in me, and I in thee, that they also may be one in us: that the world may believe that thou hast sent me. And the glory which thou gavest me I have given them; that they may be one, even as we are one: I in them, and thou in me, that they may be made perfect in one; and that the world may know that thou hast sent me, and hast loved them, as thou hast loved me. Father, I will that they also, whom thou hast given me, be with me where I am; that they may behold my glory, which thou hast

Are you praying for your children for today and for their future?

given me: for thou lovedst me before the foundation of the world. O righteous Father, the world hath not known thee: but I have known thee, and these have known that thou hast sent me. And I have declared unto them thy name, and will declare it: that the love wherewith thou hast loved me may be in them, and I in them" (John 17:1-26).

Jesus did not have to come here. He did not have to leave His throne in heaven to come to this world of darkness and sin. Yet His love would not allow Him not to come. Jesus knew when He came what the end results would be, and He still came.

The days of Jesus' ministry spent upon this earth were days of teaching, miracles, and healings. He spent His nights in prayer to the Father, and His prayers were for each of us.

When you read the prayer of Jesus in John 17, did

you feel the prayer of a Father for His children? Are you praying for your children in the love of Jesus? Are you praying for your children for today and for their future? We must pray for them today, and we must pray for what they will encounter in the future, their schooling, their career, their future spouse, and your future grandchildren. When the hard decisions come their way, will they know who to turn to for the answer? When life deals them defeat, will they know to reach out to the hand of Jesus, so He can pull them back up? Will they know His voice?

"Satan's influence is constantly exerted upon men to distract the senses, control the mind for evil, and incite to violence and crime. He weakens the body, darkens the intellect, and debases the soul. Whenever men reject the Saviour's invitation, they are yielding themselves to Satan. Multitudes in every department in life, in the home, in business, and even in the church, are doing this today. It is because of this that violence and crime have overspread the earth, and moral darkness, like the pall of death, enshrouds the habitations of men. Through his specious temptations Satan leads men to worse and worse evils, till utter depravity and ruin are the result. The only safeguard against his power is found in the presence of Jesus. Before men and angels Satan has been revealed as man's enemy and destroyer; Christ, as man's friend and deliverer. His Spirit will develop in man all that will ennoble the character and dignify the nature. It will build man up for the glory of God in body and soul and spirit" (Ellen G. White, *The Desire of Ages*, p. 341).

Chapter Twelve

He sat with his arm around his wife. He looked at her and then their two boys. He couldn't believe how quietly they sat listening to the pastor. He was so proud of them. He looked at his wife, knowing she was the reason why the boys were the way they were, because his job had never let him be there for them. But that was changing now. As he sat there, his mind wandered to that morning on that dark highway. He had been so close to leaving his family all alone that morning. Tears filled his eyes at the thought of them being all alone. He wiped them away. He looked to his wife again, who was looking back at him. She reached up and wiped a tear that had slid down his cheek, and she smiled. He felt a peace enter his heart that he had never felt.

An older man sat near the young couple. The older man was holding his wife close to him. Never in their thirty-eight years of marriage had they sat in a church for any reason other than for a wedding or a funeral. And beside them were their neighbors. The nicest people he had ever met. He had sat thinking of them the past couple of days wondering how they could have known that he and his wife had hit the bottom and had nowhere left to go. He looked to his left at the man and his wife and two boys. He could see the tears in the eyes of the man. He looked back to the pastor and listened to the words he was saying, and he found his own tears running down his cheeks. He looked to his wife and saw her tears. As his tears flowed, his heart responded to the pastor and to the name of Jesus. It seemed as each tear ran down his cheek the weight on his shoulders lifted a little, and then a little more. In his arms he could feel his wife relaxing, and he knew she was feeling the same thing.

The young man sat in the back pew with his neighbor who had invited him to come. He wanted to sit in the back in case his son started to cry, that way he could get out easily without disturbing anyone, but his son was not making a sound. It seemed, in fact, that the baby was listening. And so was he. He didn't know what was happening, but something had changed that day he had entered his neighbor's apartment. He looked down at his son who was looking directly into his eyes.

The pastor was telling a story about Jesus and a time when He had fallen asleep in a ship as a storm raged. He told of the fear of the disciples and how in their fear they had run to Jesus.

The pastor then read the following quote from *The Desire of Ages*: "When Jesus was awakened to meet the storm, He was in perfect peace. There was no trace of fear in word or look, for no fear was in His heart. But He rested not in the possession of almighty power. It was not as the 'Master of earth and sea and sky' that

He reposed in quiet. That power He had laid down, and He says, 'I can of Mine own self do nothing.' John 5:30. He trusted in the Father's might. It was in faith—faith in God's love and care—that Jesus rested, and the power of that word which stilled the storm was the power of God.

"As Jesus rested by faith in the Father's care, so we are to rest in the care of our Saviour. If the disciples had trusted in Him, they would have been kept in peace. Their fear in the time of danger revealed their unbelief. In their efforts to save themselves, they forgot Jesus; and it was only when, in despair of self-dependence, they turned to Him that He could give them help.

"How often the disciples' experience is ours! When the tempests of temptation gather, and the fierce lightnings flash, and the waves sweep over us, we battle with the storm alone, forgetting that there is One who can help us. We trust to our own strength till our hope is lost, and we are ready to perish. Then we remember Jesus, and if we call upon Him to save us, we shall not cry in vain. Though He sorrowfully reproves our unbelief and self-confidence, He never fails to give us the help we need. Whether on the land or on the sea, if we have the Saviour in our hearts, there is no need of fear. Living faith in the Redeemer will smooth the sea of life, and will deliver us from danger in the way that He knows to be best" (Ellen G. White, p. 336).

The pastor looked out to those sitting in the pews and asked, "What do you do when you are scared?"

He paused, and then said, "Jesus is waiting for you to say, as the disciples said in Matthew 8:25, 'Lord, save us: we perish.'" The pastor paused again as he closed his Bible and walked the two steps down to the level of those who sat in the pews.

"My appeal to each of you this morning is this. Each of you is here for a reason. Something or someone has brought you here. In other words, there has been an invitation."

His eyes fell across the church.

"How many of you are hearing those words inside of you right now. The words Lord save me, I perish?"

Jesus is calling.

He continued. "If you are hearing those words, your heart is calling out to Jesus and you need to respond to the call. My appeal to you is to stand to your feet and make your way to the front. Jesus is calling you."

The married man stood and took the hand of his wife, and she stood beside him. They turned to their boys and each of them grabbed a hand. Jesus was calling.

The older gentleman stood and held his hand out to his wife. She looked up at him with tears streaming down her cheeks. He thought to himself that she had never looked so beautiful. She stood to her feet. Jesus was calling.

The young man stood, holding his son in his arms.

His son had not stopped looking at him, and as he came to his feet, his son smiled at him. Jesus was calling.

Jesus is calling.

Chapter Thirteen

These have been stories of the lost and the living. To find and follow the truth that is Jesus Christ is to live, but it is at a cost. You will have to give up your life and your plans. You must die to self to resurrect in the true life that Jesus Christ has paid for with His life. When you make a choice, there must be certainty, because there is always danger in regret of poor choices.

It is not a choice that all will make, and those who do choose to accept the invitation of our Lord Jesus and follow His path will face obstacles in their lives. There will be trials and tribulations, and they will face mockery and ridicule. However, listen to the Words of Jesus.

"These things I have spoken unto you, that in me ye might have peace. In the world ye shall have tribulation: but be of good cheer; I have overcome the world" (John 16:33).

Lot, his wife, and their two daughters were spared from the fate of Sodom and Gomorrah. They were hurried out of the city before the rain of fire from God came down upon the cities. Sadly, there are those who tag along with those who have made the choice for Jesus while not actually choosing for themselves, or maybe they just had a religious experience, but the sin in their lives was calling them back. If you make a true and sincere choice, you will not look back. If you regret your choice, you will long to return to your sin and turn back. Lot and his family were told not to turn back and look at the events unfolding behind them. Those who choose Jesus Christ follow His word and never lose sight

If you make a true and sincere choice, you will not look back.

of Him. Those who don't will not heed His word or hear His voice. Something in Lot's wife—regret of losing the life she was used to or missing some sort of pleasure of sin—made her turn back and look, and at that moment she was turned into a pillar of salt. She was blind to the truth in front of her, and she looked back to the world she loved (read the whole story in Gen. 19).

"But still there are many who refuse to obey His word, because obedience would involve the sacrifice of some worldly interest. Lest His presence shall cause them pecuniary loss, many reject His grace, and drive His Spirit away" (Ellen G. White, *The Desire of Ages*, p. 339).

"And he said, Go forth, and stand upon the mount before the LORD. And, behold, the LORD passed by, and a great and strong wind rent the mountains, and brake in pieces the rocks before the LORD; but the LORD was not in the wind: and after the wind an earthquake; but the LORD was not in the earthquake: And after the earthquake a fire; but the LORD was not in the fire: and after the fire a still small voice" (1 Kings 19:11, 12).

It is that "still small voice" that saves us from the chaos surrounding us. If we listen, we can hear it, and if we open our eyes, we can see it. He has walked into our lives and cast His shadow across it. It is His hand reaching out, and His words ring in our ears, "Wilt thou be made whole?"

The voice of God could be an inaudible voice inside your heart, the words of a caring neighbor, or His hands upon you leading you into His will. He approaches each of us as only He knows how. God knows us, and when He calls, it is in a way He knows we will respond best to. He is calling. Are you listening?